Up, Up, and Away

Ginger Wadsworth

Illustrated by Patricia J. Wynne

Charlesbridge

With special thanks to E. B. White for bringing us the one-and-only Charlotte—G. W.

In memory of Garth Williams, Sam Howard, Ole Risom, and Ted Riley, who spun magic—P. J. W.

The author would like to thank Louis N. Sorkin, arachnologist at the American Museum of Natural History, for his invaluable advice.

Published by Charlesbridge
85 Main Street
Watertown, MA 02472
(617) 926-0329
www.charlesbridge.com

Library of Congress Cataloging-in-Publication Data
Wadsworth, Ginger.
    Up, up, and away / Ginger Wadsworth ; Illustrated by Patricia J. Wynne.
       p. cm.
    ISBN 978-1-58089-221-6 (reinforced for library use)
    ISBN 978-1-58089-222-3 (softcover)
1. Spiders—Juvenile literature. I. Wynne, Patricia, ill. II. Title.
QL458.4.G56 2009
595.4'4—dc22   2008040752

Printed in China
(hc) 10 9 8 7 6 5 4 3 2 1
(sc) 10 9 8 7 6 5 4 3 2 1

Illustrations done in watercolor, gouache, ink, and colored pencil on Arches hot-press watercolor paper
Display type and text type set in Ogre and Humper
Color separations by Chroma Graphics, Singapore
Printed and bound by Jade Productions
Production supervision by Brian G. Walker
Designed by Martha MacLeod Sikkema

After laying her eggs,
a mother spider wraps them
round and round
with her strong silk thread.
Then she ties her egg sac tight to a twig.

Inside the sac,

the eggs hatch.

Hundreds of sisters and brothers snuggle inside:

tiny spiderlings waiting . . .

waiting for spring.

When the warm winds blow,
baby spiders chew and chew
to make a hole in the sac.
One sister's skinny, long legs
wiggle and push,
wiggle and push,
as she tries to escape.

Finally this sister spider spills out,
followed by her siblings,
tiny dots almost too small to see.
Hungry spiderlings wobble into the welcoming sun.

After such a long wait,
Spider is ready to be free,
to stretch out each leg
and explore a new place.
But it isn't to be . . . just yet.

A long, lean lizard skids into the sun.
It leaps and lunges,
snatching up spiders for lunch.

Spider skedaddles,
but the lizard is swift.
A brisk breeze blows Spider away
just in time.

Eight legs thrash
as she turns and jerks,
until she jams to a stop on top of a rock.

Ever so quickly
Spider grabs tight
and spins a dragline,
one sturdy silk thread
to tie her to her rock.

All around her,
dozens of spiders bounce up and down
like tiny yo-yos.
Sisters dangle with sisters.
Brothers bustle over bushes.
Teeny spiderlings scurry-hurry everywhere.

The army of spiders spreads out
to hungrily hunt for food.
Here, there, and everywhere
they build quick webs
and wait.
Spider slips past siblings,
through the fast-growing city of webs.
Behind her,
a brother crunches a sister for lunch!

Into this family clash,
a bluebird swoops low,
seeking an easy snack.
Spider rappels off her rock
and escapes into a crack to hide.

Spider is hungry, so hungry,
and ready to grow.
Out she finally comes,
one leg up, one leg down,
toddling on delicate legs,
eager to start her own web
and dine on whatever drops by.

Unfortunately
there are still too many spiders
and not enough to munch.
It's time for Spider and family to scatter,
to search for homes of their own.

On this warm, windy day,
up, up Spider and her siblings climb.
Arachnids are everywhere,
on top of their world.

Spider stands on tiptoe,
bottom up.
She spins out silken thread
into the breeze.

At first

the silk thread wobbles in the wind.

But then it floats upward,

pulling Spider free.

Her legs tickle the tips of tulips

until the thread lifts her

up, up, and away with the warm wind.

Around Spider,
eight-legged kites rise.
Ballooning spiders fill the sky,
sisters and brothers drifting this way and that,
to hunt for new homes.

Then Spider soars
all alone,
hanging on to her strong, silvery string
for her very own ride.

As light as a puff of pollen,
Spider floats free.
Her eight dainty legs dangle
and dance in the wind.
At least for now,
Spider is nobody's supper
as she catches an air current
and sails out to sea.

As day turns to dusk,
the cooling air changes course,
blowing softly,
sending Spider back to land.
Gentle winds guide Spider down,
oh, so s-l-o-w-l-y,
like a balloon running out of air.

At first she strays over a stream,
then swings and twirls
right past an apple tree
near a big red barn.
Finally she lands atop a fence post.
A tasty-looking fly buzzes by,
and Spider,
hungry Spider,
decides to stay.

Without taking a single lesson,
she knows just what to do.
As the sun sets,
Spider reels out her silver thread.
She scurries
up and down
and sidesteps back and forth.

Finally she zigzags lines
through the middle of her design,
making her web just right.
Spider is home at last.

There,
near the big red barn,
Spider spends her spring and summer,
spinning webs
with tough, sticky strands
to trap insects big and small.
She bites her prey with powerful jaws
and sucks up juicy beetle guts
or sips fly stew.

Spider knows
it is important to eat,
to grow big and strong,
to meet and mate
before the fall days come.

As winter draws near,
cold air whirls around.
Spider lays her eggs
one by one
and wraps them in a silken sac.
She ties the sac tight,
then dies,
as mother spiders do every year.

All winter long,
sturdy silk threads
hold Spider's sac safe
until, inside the sac,
the eggs hatch.

Once again
hundreds of sisters and brothers
snuggle inside:
tiny spiderlings waiting . . .
waiting for spring.

When the warm winds blow,
baby spiders chew and chew
to make a hole in the sac.
One brother's skinny, long legs
wiggle and push,
wiggle and push,
as he tries to escape.
Finally this brother spider spills out first,
followed by a river of spiderlings.

He is hungry, so hungry,
ready to eat,
ready to grow,
ready to soar,
up, up, and away.

The Spin on Garden Spiders

The spider in this story is an *Argiope aurantia* (ar-GYE-oh-pee aw-RAN-tee-ah), a type of garden spider. It is also called a zipper or writing spider because of the zigzag pattern in the middle of its web. The female spider, including her eight hairy legs, is usually about an inch across. Her striking black and yellow markings develop gradually as she matures. The male is much smaller with more muted coloring. Both are harmless to people.

Garden spiders can be found in backyards and parks over much of North America. In the spring tiny spiderlings emerge from a silken egg sac. There might be just a few or several hundred babies in the sac.

To find a home of its own, a spider might hitch a ride on the wind. The spider releases liquid silk from the spinnerets at the rear of its abdomen. Air currents pull the silk out and cause it to harden. Still attached to the thread, the spider might balloon over a lake or mountain, soar to the top of a tall building, or float a short distance . . . wherever the wind blows.

A garden spider usually lives a year or less. During this busy time, it captures and eats hundreds of insects. As fall approaches, the female mates. She wraps her eggs in a sturdy silk sac, then guards it until she dies. Winter brings colder weather, and the male dies, too. But by spring new spiderlings hatch, and without their parents' help, they start the life cycle once again.